Chimpanzee

Series "Fun Facts on Zoo Animals for Kids"

Written by Michelle Hawkins

Chimpanzee

Series "Fun Facts on Zoo Animals for Kids"

By: Michelle Hawkins

Version 1.1 ~April 2021

Published by Michelle Hawkins at KDP

All information in this book has been carefully researched and checked for factual accuracy. However, the author and publisher make no warranty, express or implied, that the information contained herein is appropriate for every individual, situation, or purpose and assume no responsibility for errors or omissions.

The reader assumes the risk and full responsibility for all actions. The author will not be held responsible for any loss or damage, whether consequential, incidental, special or otherwise, that may result from the information presented in this book.

All images are free for use or purchased from stock photo sites or royalty-free for commercial use. I have relied on my own observations as well as many different sources for this book, and I have done my best to check facts and give credit where it is due. In the event that any material is used without proper permission, please contact me so that the oversight can be corrected.

Chimpanzees are only found in Central and West Africa.

Chimpanzees will use all four of their limbs to get from place to place.

Chimpanzees are considered to be endangered.

The hand of a Chimpanzee is like a human hand with a thumb as a different finger.

Chimpanzees are considered to be a purposeful pointer; they point to what they want.

Chimpanzees have a very stable personality.

By grooming each other, Chimpanzees will socially integrate themselves into the group.

Chimpanzees will, on average, sleep between eight to nine hours per night.

Chimpanzees can be very susceptible to the Ebola virus.

Chimpanzees can get the same disease that humans can get, such as measles, the common cold, and influenza.

Chimpanzees can not swim.

The average weight of a Chimpanzee is between 70 to 140 pounds.

The mom Chimpanzee will carry her baby on her back for up to four years.

Unfortunately, Chimpanzees have been used as laboratory animals.

The nest of a Chimpanzee is cleaner than a humans bed due to them rebuilding it nightly.

The Chimpanzees are not monkeys but Apes because they do not have a tail.

The dominant male of the tribe is considered the alpha male.

Chimpanzees groom each other to keep themselves healthy.

The hair on a Chimpanzee is long and dark.

Chimpanzees will only use their nest in the trees for one night and change locations the next night.

Chimpanzees will attack each other for food and mates.

Chimpanzees will pick out dirt and bugs from each other's fur.

The average height of a Chimpanzee is between four to five feet tall.

Chimpanzees are considered very clean animals.

Chimpanzees live in forests, grasslands, rainforests, and woods.

Chimpanzees will warn each other through sounds of the incoming danger.

Male Chimpanzees mature around the age of fifteen.

Chimpanzees will live together in groups of up to 150.

Chimpanzees can run up to twenty-five miles per hour.

The four types of Chimpanzees are the Central Chimpanzee, Western Chimpanzee, Eastern Chimpanzees, and the Nigeria-Cameroon Chimpanzee.

Chimpanzees will use sticks or tools to find food, such as termites.

All faces of Chimpanzees are unique.

Chimpanzees can walk on two legs with ease if they so desire.

By grooming each other, Chimpanzees form close bonds.

Chimpanzees only eat about 2% meat; the rest is in fruits and vegetables.

Chimpanzees eat most of their meals in trees.

To communicate, Chimpanzees will bark, drum, or pant.

Chimpanzees can laugh.

Chimpanzees will run, swing, or walk up to six miles per day.

When baby Chimpanzees are bored, they will make up games to play.

When Chimpanzees get sick, they will eat medicinal plants to be able to heal themselves.

The Ugandan Ironwood Tree is the tree that Chimpanzees enjoy sleeping in the most.

Male Chimpanzees will stay with the group that they are born into.

Chimpanzees will not make good pets because they can become aggressive.

Chimpanzees have a wide mouth.

Chimpanzees are seven times stronger than humans.

Chimpanzees can walk on two legs.

Chimpanzees walk on all four of their limbs; this is called knuckle-walking.

Chimpanzees are found in twenty different countries in Africa.

The way that Chimpanzees travel the most is by their arms.

Chimpanzees are endangered due to their habitat and food loss.

Chimpanzees do not have a tail.

Chimpanzees have flat faces
with big eyes.

When Chimpanzees are children,
they are very affectionate.

Chimpanzees are considered one of the most intelligent animals.

Chimpanzees have the same five senses that humans do; hear, sight, smell, taste, and touch.

Female Chimpanzees mature around the age of thirteen.

Grooming will help to calm over-excited Chimpanzees.

Chimpanzees will play games as a four-year-old would.

Chimpanzees use over fifty different gestures to communicate.

Chimpanzees will use rocks to help open nuts.

Chimpanzees' average life span is between forty to fifty in the wild and sixty in captivity.

Chimpanzee's nests are built out of branches and leaves.

Chimpanzees enjoy hugging and kissing each other as a sign of communication.

When you see a Chimpanzee smile, it is a grimace of fear.

Chimpanzees communicate through gestures and facial expressions.

Baby Chimpanzees are born with white on their tail but will disappear before adulthood.

A Chimpanzees long hands and fingers help them to climb trees and swing.

Mom and child Chimpanzee are always close.

Chimpanzees can get Alzheimer's disease.

Baby Chimpanzees will spend their first two years on their mother's back.

Female Chimpanzees will leave the group that they are born into and find another group to join.

Chimpanzees have black fur till they are older when their fur turns gray.

Female Chimpanzees are very trusting but timid.

Chimpanzees have the ability to learn sign language.

During a female Chimpanzees entire life, they will only have three children.

There are less than 200,000 Chimpanzees left in the world.

Chimpanzees are considered omnivores where they eat most fruits and plants with an occasional frog and lizard.

A group of Chimpanzees is called a community.

Chimpanzees are considered to be very social.

Chimpanzees will sleep in trees, in nests that they make nightly.

Chimpanzees have a hard time swimming due to their long arms and short legs.

During the first six months of life, baby Chimpanzees are carried on their mother's stomach.

A Chimpanzees's nest is made
up of leaves.

Chimpanzees can feel empathy
toward others.

Chimpanzees and Bonobos are
the closest relative to humans.

Find me on Amazon at:

https://amzn.to/3oqoXoG

and on Facebook at:

https://bit.ly/3ovFJ5V

Other Books by Michelle Hawkins

Series

Fun Facts on Birds for Kids.

Fun Fact on Fruits and Vegetables

Fun Facts on Small Animals

Fun Facts on Dogs for Kids.

Fun Facts on Dates for Kids.

Fun Facts on Zoo Animals for Kids.

Made in the USA
Monee, IL
20 December 2022

22969115R10021